Shall I Go On?

Brendan White

BookLeaf
Publishing

India | USA | UK

Presentation by *BookLeaf Publishing*

Web: www.bookleafpub.com

E-mail: info@bookleafpub.com

ISBN: 9789360940430

First edition 2024

To:

*The Whites, funding my life while I write my
way through it*

And every eye to grace these pages,

You are loved.

ACKNOWLEDGEMENT

Lady K, who has exposed me to many of my own faults.
EB King, my fellow foot soldier in life

PREFACE

Change is essential to the way we find excellence.

To Confess

1

To Trust you is My Blessing.
To Recognise this is a Luxury.
The fear it volleys from chamber to chamber
in my heart shows me how human I am.
I Love to Learn to Love within your care
It's a Blessing.
Understanding this fact is my Luxury.

Thank you.

Kiss by Kiss

By the time we make it to the bed,
We'll have shared a dozen kisses.
Each one more powerfully pushing us deeper
into intimacy's clutches
By the time we're wed,
We'll have shared a thousand kisses.
Peck by Peck, our lips become our mode of
communication.
By the time we're dead,
We'll have shared the taste of our two lives
conjoined
Our tongues are two
Our speech now one.
With every pressed together moment shared,
We teach ourselves to
Speak
with one language
Taste
with one palate
Love
with one intention.

Kiss by Kiss.

?

3

Can one find joy in futility?
Do we accept the mundane grind of daily life?
Is one happier when devoid of ambition?
Is it harder to try to want something you may
never have than to embrace something you will
never desire?

Pity the Perpetrators

Imagine my sentiments
That I have towards
Myself are just Re-
Flections of the
Feelings present
Towards this wretched world.
I'd not be surprised to find
My self loathing courting my distrust,
Being coaxed into relations with the resentment
Dwelling deep in the pits of my midst.
How scary the feeling is
That the cone of my vision
May be painted by the harsh inked words
Spilled in my presence.

Pity the Perpetrators
Be Kind To Yourself

In Perpetuity.

5

As I lay sand-eyed and stenched
With the taste of the night on my tongue,
The clock past noon upon my day's arrival,
Traces of you pressed against my now cracked
lips,
I warp to times of lush life
With you in my arms,
The aroma of romance,
The delicacy you call skin,
The glide of hand and leg,
As the present loathes the past,
My heart marries the future,
In Perpetuity.

Hold On Not

Though the shoe no longer fits
Memories of how it once did have chained it to
the closet floor.
As it is weighed down by the many others
New and Old
It becomes acquainted with the dust and mold
Mending it to the mound so closely that
Individuality is no longer a factor.
Now,
The shoes and shirts
Shawls, Skirts
That once fit who no longer exists,
Have become a metamorphic force
Causing short breath and sickness.
The root no longer identifiable
One is forced to bear the task of removing it all
at once,
Removing every sticky, stubborn article
One from another.
Chiseling, Burning
Risking the loss of their own self inside
This mass of past
Kept in wraps.

Throw away the shoes as soon as they do not fit.
For you.

Sisyphus

Sometimes
It
Seems
You
Push
Heaven
Upon
Seas

How do you stay happy?
Find purpose.
For once you reach your goals,
What's left?
Purpose cannot be achieved.
Pursue the impact of a constant work.
Whatever you do,
Don't stop pushing

Don't Try, Do.

To be so caught up in your effort,
You don't consider it might be misplaced.
To be so caught up in your effort,
You don't see the your counterpart succeed.
To be so caught up in your effort,
You don't focus on your tactic.
To be so caught up in your effort,
You don't see it doesn't read.
To be so caught up in your effort,
Precision suffers for lack of attention.
To be so caught up in your effort,
Perception says you're the only one exerting.
To be so caught up in your effort,
Praise is due for just the trying.
To be so caught up in your effort,
People close to you get hurt.

the sun was our signal

9

The sun was our signal
The sky turning light
Marked the ending of beginnings
As we stretched through the night
Our newfound expressions
And longsought connection
The sun was our signal
We're doing things right
It must be the basis
Of lover's foundation
We lay through the way
We kiss in slow paces
Reminding our minds
Not to rush into pavement
But soar,
We've been gifted a blessed arrangement

Let the sun be the light
Let our hearts share the glow.

Do U Know?

10

Let's strip away your world
You've never experienced anything
Never felt a insult or a compliment
Never seen a mountain or a dumpster
There's been no love or grief
No joy or fear
Say you never touched society or nature,

Who are you?

Reaching For

My greatest joy is in pursuit
To go and to know
You're headed somewhere
Towards Zen
Towards Truth
Towards Wisdom
Towards Youth
Towards Heaven
Towards You

I may never reach
The things I reach toward
But the days teach me most
When in each I inch forward

The Fact Remains

12

I fear as I long
In each tear lies hope
It takes bliss to rile my anger
I would not
Waste a Fume
Where I see no Fertility

The fact remains:
To love is to suffer.

Traffic Love

13

I've never been so comforted by traffic before,
But we're all trying to get somewhere that the
6 cars within a
4 foot radius are
not privy to,
Looking for creative ways to get ourselves out
of the jam,
Careful not to crash into other people's journey,
The occasional courtesy to let someone over
Because you know
That you will reach
Your destination in time,
After two decades,
I really learn how to enjoy the journey.

Take your time,
Love the traffic.

In Love Alone

Is loving suffering?
Is loving a ticket to an early grave?
Do we ever truly love?
Do we know how?
What is sacrifice?
What is giving more than you get?
How do you forfeit your desires for someone
else's?
How do you wire your brain to receive pain so
there is comfort elsewhere?
Can we self sufficient balls of flesh maintain this
level of self-compromise?
Can we even achieve it momentarily?
For a minute?
For the right person?
Our family?
Ourselves?

Is love killing us slowly?
Or loving alone?

But, I Love

I hate them all.
I hate that they saw parts of you they did not
deserve to.
I hate that you wanted with them what you have
with me.
I hate that they treated you as less than you are.
I hate that you treated you as less than you are.
I hate that they touched you.
I hate that they kissed you.
I hate that you thought you wanted them to.
I hate that you're still affected by the experience.
I hate that they left me with such a broken
version of you.

But, I love you enough to help piece you back
together again.

Faith Without Works

Keep me in your sight,
Though at times
I've shut mine eyes to thee,
Forgive me my distrust,
In spite of my refusal,
Teach me right,
Though at times
I prefer to be wrong,
Purge from me my lusts,
Ignoring my abuses,
Comfort my mind
And grant me peace,
Though I have
Always chosen tumult...

How would you respond to this request?

To the Brightest of Black

Deliver me your worries,
I will show you protection.
Give me your pain,
I will show you strength.
Expose to me your flaws,
I will show you art.
Tell me your ignorances,
I will show you curiosity.
Lend me your darkness,
I will return light.

S&M

Woe is the unconquered mind,
For this relinquishes the power to decide
to the Heart,
Which concedes its duty of feeling
to the Skin,
Who serves the purpose of reacting
to its Environment,

To not take control of the mind
is to allow something else to.
Choose your master,
Or you will forever be a slave.

Light

Light Leaks on Night Streets
No Lampposts, but High Peaks
In Distance while Tai Chi
Waved Patrons Ignite Tea
Water for the Upright Teen
That won't Chase the Night's Gleam
But Runs toward a Bright Dream
And Simple though it Might Seem
It's Hard to Stitch such Tight Seams
With Tempting Clips of Fight Scenes
And Pipe Fiends and Fright Things
I Thank God for the Light Beams
Reminding us that Light Beams

Abby Singer

This is My Retreat
You've Trusted Me With Your Time
Thus Making Me Full

TYFLM

21

Lovers of the past
Left me all in pieces
So thank you for leaving me with peace.

9 789360 940430